2022

Mexico City

The Restaurant Enthusiast's
Discriminating Guide

Andrew Delaplaine

Andrew Delaplaine is the Food Enthusiast.
When he's not playing tennis,
he dines anonymously
at the Publisher's (considerable) expense.

James Cubby – Senior Editor

The Restaurant Enthusiast's Discriminating Guide

Table of Contents

INTRODUCTION

I love Mexico City, even though the first time I traveled there, with my mother, we almost brought her back in a box. She had made the mistake of using the ice cubes in her hotel room fridge to make a drink instead of pouring bottled water into the ice trays.

Boom!

You're sick as a dog.

But that was many years ago. Generally, I've had nothing but wonderful times in Mexico City.

When I think about what Mexico City was and how it came to be what it is today, my mind still boggles.

You have to remember that the whole city is built on a drained lake bed. When there was still a lake, around 1325, it was established as the Aztec capital called Tenochititlán. The island in the middle of the lake was reached by way of a series of causeways. This was what Hernan Cortes found when he showed up in 1521. He promptly destroyed it.

Mexico has a rich and bloody history, not unlike all the other countries in the New World where the indigenous populations where slaughtered or enslaved. (But one has to remember that Cortes didn't do anything to the Aztecs that the English settlers didn't do to the Indians.)

The altitude is high, over 7,000 feet, so if you come from a low-lying coastal area, be prepared for some difficulty in breathing. And while the government has made enormous strides in cleaning up the famously polluted air in Mexico City, it's still pretty awful. You have to pray for good air. But you can never be sure of it.

There are things about Mexico in general that you want to be aware of if you want to travel wisely—and safely. The State Department says 14 of the 31 states (and Federal District, or *Distrito Federal*, or D.F., which is Mexico City) have no travel warnings. The others you want to avoid because of the drug-related gang warfare that's an ongoing reality in Mexico, responsible for ripping the country apart. (Americans are really to blame, since we're the ones buying all the drugs.)

One of the reasons Mexico City is so much more safe than other parts of the country is that everybody wants to be able to come here and visit it in peace, and this includes a lot of the high-end drug dealers, many of whom have houses and families here. They don't want to come here and duel it out on the streets the way they do elsewhere.

Of the 20 top foreign locations for Americans, 4 are in Mexico: No. 2 is Cancun, followed by No. 3, Playa del Carmen, Cabo san Lucas / Los Cabos at No. 11 and Puerto Vallarta at No. 15.

One good thing about Mexico City is that it has been sidestepped by the drug cartels so there's no sense of the overwhelming violence that occurs in other parts of Mexico.

You will find the *Distrito Federal* (Federal District, another name for the city) to be quite a beautiful, handsomely laid-out city.

Lay of the Land

At 571 square miles, D.F.—as Mexico City residents, or *chilangos*, call it—is vast, but visitors gravitate to a few key neighborhoods.

Centro Histórico: Anchored by the Zócalo plaza, the historic center is a mix of monuments and bustling commerce.

Roma: Hipsters, artists, and boutique owners have revived this once-bourgeois neighborhood of Art Nouveau mansions.

Condesa: In Mexico City's answer to New York's West Village, shops, restaurants, and apartments radiate out from the Parque México.

Polanco: One of the city's poshest districts keeps expanding north: "Nuevo Polanco" is being colonized by galleries and shopping malls.

Getting Around Safely: Taxis are plentiful, but you may feel more secure having a private car. From Journey Mexico at www.journeymexico.com

For the latest safety information, go to the U.S. State Department at travel.state.gov.

CASH & DEBIT CARDS.

Notify the companies whose cards you use that you are going to Mexico. Transactions might be blocked if you don't. Have them send you alerts or call you if any charge looks suspicious. When using ATMs, try to avoid street side ATMs in favor of ATMS inside a bank or other business.

Have credit card numbers and other information written down in a safe place.

You'll need cash because a lot of places don't accept plastic. But get your currency converted before going to Mexico because you'll stick out as a foreigner by getting it done at the airport when you land. (The rates are high there too.) A lot of currency exchange booths are not in secure areas, so beware.

YOUR DRESS.

You're not in Vegas, you're in a potentially dangerous city, so leave the shorts and flip-flops at home unless you're visiting the beach somewhere. Don't be an obvious tourist. Keep your camera in your travel bag, not around your neck.

YOUR PHONE.

Don't be glued to it the way so many people are, not when you're out on the streets. You're begging for trouble.

Check with your carrier to find out what the fees are when traveling in Mexico.

GETTING ABOUT

UBER
https://www.uber.com/global/en/cities/mexico-city/

Helpful tips from Uber

There's an extensive Metro system, a bus system, a trolley system. I would avoid them all unless you *really* know your way around. I never use them. Never.

They even have special cars on the Metro system for women only because women get groped on the mixed cars. Also there's the constant threat of pickpockets. Stay away.

Mexico City is one of the world's largest cities and boasts an estimated population of 21 million people living in the region. Mexico City is divided into 16 areas known as delegaciones, not unlike New York's boroughs. These areas are further divided into neighborhoods called "colonias" and there are about 250 of these.

When traveling the city, it is important to know which colonia that you're traveling to and be aware that some have duplicate or very similar names. Visitors to Mexico City need to take note of the increase in crime and safety concerns that are prevalent in the city.

While traveling throughout Mexico City by public transportation can be economical, it is not always the safest mode of transportation and warnings regarding use of public transportation should be respected.

Locals and those familiar with Mexico City travel freely and cheaply via the Metro, first- and second-class buses.

However, visitors should travel by ***sitio taxis*** (official taxis registered to a specific locale or hotel), as these taxis are fairly inexpensive and the safest means of travel within the city.

"Turismo" and Sitio Taxis

These two methods are the safest means of travel within Mexico City. Turismo taxis, un-marked cabs, are usually luxury cars that are assigned to specific hotels and are identified by their special license plates. These may be more expensive that other taxis but they are the safest.

Established rates are fixed for travel to and from the airport. However, rates for traveling to other destinations and sightseeing need to be negotiated with the drivers.

The bell captain at your hotel can tell you what the airport fare should be and make sure to confirm with the cab driver before departure. Theses cab drivers, usually licensed English-speaking guides, can be excellent tour guides and provide valuable information regarding Mexico City.

While these cabs usually charge around 15% more than metered rates, the price is well worth it as these drivers can wait for you while you dine or shop or will pick you up when you call.

Getting Around Safely: Taxis are plentiful, but you may feel more secure having a private car. From Journey Mexico at www.journeymexico.com

Metered Taxis

Some sitio taxis (radio taxis) are safe and use meters, others have fixed rates. Travelers need to be cautious as some drivers will overcharge passengers, advance the meter, or even drive farther than requested to run up the tab.

Do not hail a taxi. A lot of the drivers are unlicensed, illegal and unsafe.

Your hotel will call a reputable taxi for you, a "radio taxi." If you're in a restaurant and ready to leave at night, have them call a cab for you.

If you're out on the street and need a cab, go into a nearby hotel or restaurant and have them call for you. Or go to a taxi stand, labeled *Sitio de Taxi,* where real tcxis will be located. These are designated taxis and OK to use. These maroon and gold Nissans are slightly more expensive than the green *libre* taxis, but much more secure.

Metro

The Mexico City subway offers one of the cheapest fares in the world and has twelve lines that cover the entire city. The Metro is open Monday – Friday (5 a.m. to midnight), Saturday (6 a.m. to midnight), and Sunday (7 a.m. to midnight). The Metro is very crowded during the day and traveling during rush hours should be avoided. Tickets are sold at the ticket booth in each station. After passing through the turnstile, look for two large signs showing the destinations and follow the signs. Make sure you know where you are going as there is only one map with the routes at the entrance of the station. Note: SALIDA means EXIT and ANDENES means PLATFORMS. Once you get on the train, there's a map of the station stops for that line only located above each door. CORRESPONDENCIAS means transfer points. Be prepared to walk a bit inside the Metro system, especially when transferring lines. **Remember, this is not the safest way to travel and Metro pickpockets prey on tourists.**

Bus

Traveling by bus is common for locals. However, visitors should beware. There are bus stops on all the major tourist streets and most post a map with the full route description. The Metrobus, introduced in 2006, runs in its own designated lane up and down Avenida Insurgentes and usually travels faster than the surrounding traffic. Most of these buses are used by commuters but if you know where you're going and know the stop, the Metrobus is a better alternative to the other buses.

Microbuses

Some tourists like to use the peseros (microbuses); these are sedans or minibuses that run along major roadways. These buses have established fares and pick up and let off passengers along the route and usually offer a more comfortable ride and speedy journey. These microbuses are usually green and gray and display cards in the windshield with their routes. As the bus nears a stop, the driver will put his hand out the wind displaying one or more fingers indicating the number of passengers he can accommodate.

Tourist Bus

Many cities feature the red double-decker hop-on and hop-off tour buses (in Mexico City they are called **Turibuses;** www.turibus.com.mx and here in Mexico City they offer different tours in the north and south of the city. Each bus seats 75 and offers an audio tour in five languages. These buses operate from 9 a.m. to 9 p.m. and for a set fee tourists can hop-on and hop off as often as desired. One of their most popular tours is the Chapultepec-Centro Histórico route with 25 stops including major monuments, museums and neighborhoods. Another favorite circuit takes passengers from La Roma neighborhood south with stops that include the World Trade Center, Plaza de Torros bullring, Carillo Gil museum, Perisur shopping center, and the Frida

Kahlo museum. Another tour route goes to the pyramids at Teotihuacán.

Rental Car

If you are traveling without a car and want to travel to Puebla or other surrounding areas, you may consider a rental car. Be warned that due to the high percentage of auto theft, **renting a car in Mexico City is not recommended**.

Do not rent a car unless you're familiar with the area. These people drive like maniacs. The last thing you want is to be in a fender bender in this country where bribes are so common. If you're not prepared to deal with the police, avoid renting a car.

It is not advised to drive in the city if you're not familiar with the streets and neighborhoods, especially if you don't read Spanish, as all the signs are in Spanish, and you certainly don't want to take the chance of landing in one of the city's unsavory neighborhoods. One safe option is to hire a car with a driver—Avis offers chauffeur-driven rental cars at all of its Mexico City locations –the drivers know the area and are great tour guides. (Avis – 800-352-7900 in the U.S. or 1-800-288-8888 in Mexico).

**St Regis (center above) and the
King Cole Bar (below)**

The A to Z Listings
Ridiculously Extravagant
Sensible Alternatives
Quality Bargain Spots

One good thing about eating in Mexico City is that it's possible to eat cheaply here from one end of town to the other. The street food is really terrific, maybe the best in the world except for certain cities in Southeast Asia. Every corner will have great food on it.

TOURS-FOOD
CLUB TENGO HAMBRE
https://clubtengohambre.com/

If you find exploring the fascinating topic of Mexican cuisine a little on the daunting side, you won't be the first one to grapple with some basic fears. Should I drink the water? (Only if it's bottled.) Should I eat the food? This latter question is especially pertinent when it comes to the famous "street food" one finds on every corner in this sprawling city. A great way to deal with this, and have some fun as well, is to take one of the tours offered by this company. You'll have some wonderful experiences, and you won't be afraid to eat the food. Besides the food, you'll get an insider's guide to the city.

MEXICO CITY STREET FOOD ESSENTIALS
This walking tour takes about 3 ½ hours and makes 6 stops. They insist the places they stop to eat will serve food only available here in the city, and not in other places in the country. Interesting, right?

INSIDER'S GUIDE TO MEXICO CITY'S STREET FOOD – MARKETS + SWEETS + PULQUE
This walking tour takes between 3 and 4 hours and makes 6 stops
With this tour, they take you to the best & most interestingly varied food stands downtown, as well as markets, panaderias, confectioneries, and introduce you to pulque, which is a milk-colored drink that goes back centuries and packs a real punch. It's the fermented juice of the maguey plant (the agave plant—the blue agave is used to make tequila). It looks somewhat off-putting (even disgusting), but after the second one, you'll grow to love it. LOL.

MEXICO CITY AFTER DARK

This walking tour takes about 3 ½ hours and makes 7 stops. I really enjoyed this one, because I don't like to go out too late by myself, but this was great fun. Some food stands are best at night, and I've never had better tacos, anywhere, period. They also take you to an historic cantina and a pulqueria where you can really get soused.

AMAYA

Calle Gral. Prim 95, +01 55 5592 5671
http://www.amayamexico.com/
CUISINE: International
DRINKS: Full Bar
SERVING: Lunch & Dinner
PRICE RANGE: $$$

NEIGHBORHOOD: Juárez

Lovely little place with high ceilings and Aztec / Mayan murals painted over old red brick walls that definitely give the eatery a certain charm. A small bar has a handful of seats where you can also eat. Small but complex menu featuring dishes like: Lamp pita, Soft shell crab, and Tuna ceviche. Nice wine list focusing on natural wines. Excellent Vegetarian options.

AZUL CONDESA

Nuevo León 68, Cuauhtémoc, Hipódromo, Mexico City, +52-55-5286-6380
www.azul.rest
CUISINE: Mexican
DRINKS: Full Bar
SERVING: Breakfast, Lunch
PRICE RANGE: $$$
NEIGHBORHOOD: Condesa

Chef Ricardo Munoz Zurita offers a menu of authentic Mexican cuisine in a simple atmosphere of wooden tables and chairs. Though the dining room is electric with activity, try to get one of the tables in the atrium garden if you can swing it. Very lush and tropical. Menu favorites include: Beef drizzled in a smoky Oaxacan mole, Veracruz style fish, and ancient Mayan dishes. Try the "enigmatico" chichilo negro, which is one of the 7 Oaxaca moles you seldom see. (It's made with chihuacle pepper ashes and is usually served with beef.)

AZUL HISTÓRICO
Isabel la Católica, 30, Centro Historico A, 52 55 5510 1316
www.azul.rest
CUISINE: Mexican
DRINKS: Full Bar
SERVING: Brunch, Lunch, Dinner
PRICE RANGE: $$$
NEIGHBORHOOD: Downtown south / Centro Sur
With lights in the thick-branched trees overhead, you couldn't find a more romantic spot than this popular restaurant serving favorites like Stuffed Duck Fritters dipped in mole and Black Chichilo Chiluacle Chili served with venison. This is also a great place for breakfast, serving favorites like chilaquiles, Mexican eggs, and enchiladas. Try the delicious house-made chocolate cake served with gorgonzola cheese ice cream.

BELMONDO

Tabasco 109, Mexico City, +55 62 73 2079
www.belmondo.com.mx/
CUISINE: Deli, Sandwiches
DRINKS: Wines
SERVING: Lunch & Dinner
PRICE RANGE: $
NEIGHBORHOOD: Roma Norte
This eatery draws lots of young creative and trendy
types and offers a simple menu featuring salads,
sandwiches as spot on and good as any you've had
anywhere. Also a curated list of wines by the glass.
Menu favorites include: the French dip with roast
beef and gravy, or the grilled cheese with caramelized
onions. Closed Sundays. Be prepared for a wait.

BÓSFORO

Luis Moya 31, Mexico City, +52 55 5512 1991

No Website
CUISINE: Mexican
DRINKS: Full Bar
SERVING: Breakfast, Lunch, Dinner
PRICE RANGE: $$
NEIGHBORHOOD: Federal District
This small friendly neighborhood bar specializes in mezcales and offers a menu of Mexican bar food with favorites like the quesadilla and tapas. Try the desserts especially if you're a chocolate lover.

CABRERA 7
Calle Plaza Luis Cabrera 7, Miguel Hidalgo, Mexico City, 52 55 5264 4465
CUISINE: Mexican
DRINKS: Full Bar
SERVING: Brunch, Lunch, Dinner

PRICE RANGE: $$
NEIGHBORHOOD: Roma Norte
This superb two-level restaurant and lounge bar
(overlooking the gorgeous fountains decorating **Plaza
Luis Cabrera**), and has a menu featuring Mexican
cuisine from all regions. Menu favorites include:
Oaxacan mole, cochinita pibil, and of course the tacos
and tortas. This place makes for great people-
watching as artists set up makeshift stalls to sell their
wares and the whole population flows by in a
continuous and colorful parade of humanity.

CAFÉ EL POPULAR RESTAURANTE
5 de Mayo, No. 50-52, Mexico City, 55 5518-6081
CUISINE: Cafe
DRINKS: No Booze
SERVING: 24 hours
PRICE RANGE: $$
NEIGHBORHOOD: Central Historic District
This 24-hour café offers great Mexican breakfast like
huevos rancheros or enchiladas verdes under a wood
beamed ceiling. Great coffees and pastries. If you're
lucky there will be live music.

CAFÉ NIN
Calle Havre 73, Juárez, Mexico, +52 55 9155 4805
www.cafenin.com.mx
CUISINE: Breakfast
DRINKS: No Booze
SERVING: Breakfast
PRICE RANGE: $$
NEIGHBORHOOD: Juárez

Great choice for breakfast and the most popular brunch spot in the area. Impressive selection of baked goods – everything from doughnuts to croissants and the best-ever guava cheese pastries. Delicious cappuccino. Nice small plates as well, like the avocado & squid ceviche.

CAFÉ PASSMAR

Calle Adolfo Prieto s/n Local 237, Mexico City, +52 55 5669 1994
www.cafepassmar.com
CUISINE: Cafeteria/Coffeehouse
NEIGHBORHOOD: Benito Juárez
Just a coffeehouse that offers a full range of coffees beyond Starbucks presentation along with fruit smoothies, herbal teas, and frappes.

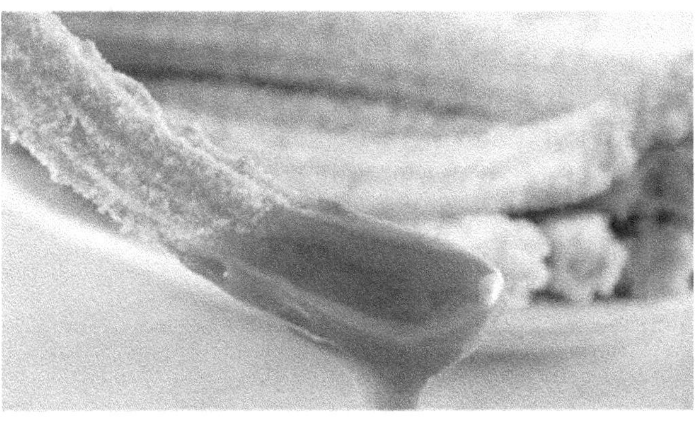

CHURRERÍA EL MORO

Several Locations (more listed on web site)
Eje Central Lázaro Cárdenas 42, Centro +52 55 5512 0896

Calle Río Lerma 167, Col. Cuauhtémoc + 52 55 5512 0896
Mercado Roma, Querétaro 225
Av. Michoacán 27, Col. Condesa
https://elmoro.mx/
CUISINE: Churros
DRINKS: No Booze
SERVING: 24 hours (some locations hours vary)
PRICE RANGE: $
NEIGHBORHOOD: Histórico, Centro / Roma Norte / Centro Sur / Condesa / Cuauhtémoc
Churros, churros, churros. Beautifully designed bakeries—light, bright and cheerful—(though the decor changes from one location to another) featuring churros, which is basically just plain dough fried and sugared. Originating in Portugal and Spain, churros are a mainstay snack here in Mexico and a lot of other Latin countries. They have to be eaten when they're warm to be fully appreciated. Here at this bakery, where they do things the old-fashioned way, they make 'em to order, so you get fresh churros with a variety of toppings, everything from deep dark chocolate to dulce de leche. Try the churro ice cream sandwiches. Impressive selection of hot chocolates.

CONTRAMAR
Calle de Durango 200, Mexico City, +52 55 5514 9217
www.contramar.com.mx **WEBSITE DOWN AT PRESSTIME**
CUISINE: Seafood
DRINKS: Full Bar
SERVING: Lunch, Dinner

PRICE RANGE: $$$
NEIGHBORHOOD: Condesa
This seafood restaurant is considered one of the chicest dining halls in the whole country, and not so much for its food, which is fine, but for the eclectic mix of artists, hipsters and trendy types it attracts. Blue and white color scheme highlights the high-ceilinged room. Best people-watching in the city. Has a great selection of dishes, including Tuna Tostadas, Oysters & pescado a la talla, Crab Cakes, and Spaghetti with Clams.

COOX HANAL

Calle Isabel la Catolica 83, Centro Histórico, Centro, 06090 Ciudad de México, CDMX,
+52 55 5709 3613 **WEBSITE DOWN AT PRESSTIME**
www.cooxhanal.com
CUISINE: Mexican
DRINKS: Full bar
SERVING: Lunch & Dinner
PRICE RANGE: $$$
NEIGHBORHOOD: Central Historic District
Popular eatery (since 1953) on the second floor offering authentic Yucatan fare like *poc chuc* (pork grilled after being marinated in orange juice). Other menu picks: Chamorro and Lime soup. Live music. This place was originally opened by boxer Raul Salazar, from Yucatan's capital, Merida.

DELIRIO

Ave. Monterrey 116-b, Mexico City, +52 55 5584 0870

www.delirio.mx

CUISINE: French/Deli

DRINKS: Beer & Wine Only

SERVING: Breakfast, Lunch & Dinner; closed Mon

PRICE RANGE: $$

NEIGHBORHOOD: Roma Norte

Great place to stop if you're looking for non-Mexican fare. Light dishes like focaccia.

DULCE PATRIA

Anatole France 100, Mexico City, 52 55 3300 3999
www.dulcepatria.mx/
CUISINE: Mexican
DRINKS: Full Bar
SERVING: Breakfast, Lunch
PRICE RANGE: $$$$
NEIGHBORHOOD: Polanco
Chef Martha Ortiz offers a menu of traditional Mexican cuisine with a modern twist. It's her innovative approach that has pushed her to the forefront of the "New Mexican" cuisine that's exploding all over the country (and abroad). This 90-seat eatery features two terraces inside the restaurant giving an outdoor feel. Definitely begin with her ceviche. But also try her fabulous "sangritas" as a chaser after you down a shot of tequila.

EL CARDENAL

Palma 23, México, D.F., +52 55 5521 3080

www.restauranteelcardenal.com
CUISINE: Mexican
DRINKS: Full Bar
SERVING: Breakfast, Lunch, & Dinner
PRICE RANGE: $$
NEIGHBORHOOD: Centro Sur
Located in a beautiful old house, this popular eatery serves authentic Mexican fare. Favorites: Quesadillas with guac, and Chicken with nopales. Popular brunch spot. If you're there for one of the best breakfast in town, get the *huevos en caldo de frijol.*

EL FAROLITO
Altata 19, Col. Condesa, México, D.F., +52-55-5273-0142
www.taqueriaselfarolito.com.mx
CUISINE: Tacos
DRINKS: No Booze
SERVING: Lunch & Dinner
PRICE RANGE: $
NEIGHBORHOOD: Condesa
Delicious Mexican fare prepared right in front of you at this decades-old spot with several locations. Try the Faroladas de Bisteck (Pita bread with steak and cheese). Nice selection of fruit juices.

EL HIDALGUENSE
Campeche 155, Mexico City, +52 55 5564 0538
No Website
CUISINE: Mexican
DRINKS: No Booze
SERVING: Open only 7 a.m. – 5 p.m. Fri - Sun
PRICE RANGE: $$

NEIGHBORHOOD: Roma Sur

A locals' favorite, this Mexican eatery offers a great selection of barbecue, meats, montalayo, and seafood. Authentic Mexican fare.

EL MAYOR

República de Argentina 15, Col. Centro, Mexico City, 52 55 5704 7580

www.restaurantelmayor.com.mx

CUISINE: Mexican

DRINKS: Full Bar

SERVING: Brunch, Lunch

PRICE RANGE: $$

NEIGHBORHOOD: Centro Histórico

Located on the top floor above a bookstore, this modern restaurant offers a menu of Mexican favorites and European-influenced fusion dishes. This is also a great place for brunch. There's a rooftop bar that overlooks the ruins of the Aztec city.

EL TURIX

Emilio Castelar, 212, Mexico City, 52 55 5280 6449
CUISINE: Mexican
DRINKS: Beer & Wine
SERVING: Lunch, Dinner
PRICE RANGE: $
NEIGHBORHOOD: Colonia Polanco
Located in a dingy storefront, but the food is worth the visit. There's an outdoor patio and a couple tables inside. Menu favorites include Cochinita pibil (pork slowly cooked with achiote that is a specialty of the Yucatán) and Tamales.

EL VENADITO

Universidad 1701, Col. Chimalistac, México, D.F.,
+52 55 5661 9786
No Web Site
CUISINE: Tacos
DRINKS: Beer &Wine
SERVING: Lunch & Dinner
PRICE RANGE: $
NEIGHBORHOOD: Florida
For over 50 years this place has served typical
Mexican fare to lines of happy customers. Known for
their great Carnitas. Favorites: Enchiladas, tacos al
pastor and French toast dessert. Across the street you
can see the Chapel of San Jose del Atillo.

ENO

Francisco Petrarca 258, Mexico City, +52 55 5531
8300
www.eno.com.mx
CUISINE: Sandwiches
DRINKS: Beer & Wine Only
SERVING: Breakfast, Lunch & Dinner
PRICE RANGE: $$
NEIGHBORHOOD: Polanco
Casual eatery that specializes in sandwiches. Great
spot for breakfast or lunch. Seating is communal.
Favorites include the carnitas de atun (seared tuna)
sandwich.

FLOR DE LIS

Avenida Mazatlan 30, Condesa, Mexico City, 52 55
5211 0060
www.tamalesyatole.com

CUISINE: Mexican
DRINKS: Beer & Wine
SERVING: Dinner
PRICE RANGE: $
NEIGHBORHOOD: Condesa
If you're looking for tamales, this is your place. There's a nice variety including chicken, peppers, beef, mole, and sweet (fruit). The atmosphere is quaint but the food is solid. Menu favorites included the Chicken and tomato tamale wrapped in banana leaf.

FONDA MARGARITA
Adolfo Prieto 1364, Mexico City, +52 55 5559 6358
CUISINE: Mexican
DRINKS: No Booze
SERVING: Breakfast, Lunch & Dinner
PRICE RANGE: $
NEIGHBORHOOD: Benito Juarez
Authentic Mexican cuisine typical of the region. Try the chicharrones in green sauce served with fresh tortillas and eggs and beans. Very few vegetarian options. Spanish speaking only.

HAVRE 77
Havre 77, Col. Juárez, México, D.F., 5208 1070
http://havre77.mx/
CUISINE: French-Mexican
DRINKS: No Booze
SERVING: Breakfast, Lunch; closed Mon & Tues
PRICE RANGE: $$$$
NEIGHBORHOOD: Juárez

Small eatery reminiscent of cafes in Paris. A perfect place to stop when you want a break from Mexican food. Favorites: Steak frites, Escargots du Jour and Laitue (salad with fresh tarragon). Delicious French pastries make this a nice stop early in the morning.

HOSTERIA DE SANTO DOMINGO
Calle Belisario Dominguez 72, 06010 México, D.F., +52 55 5510 1434
No Website
CUISINE: Mexican
DRINKS: Full bar
SERVING: Breakfast, Lunch & Dinner
PRICE RANGE: $$
NEIGHBORHOOD: Centro Norte
Traditional authentic Mexican fare in the city's oldest restaurant that opened in the 1860s. Gourmet dishes featuring meats and fish, like the *chile en nogado*, large poblano chile peppers stuffed full of ground meat, dried fruit and topped with a rich, creamy sauce. Live music. The atmosphere may remind you of your grandmother's house, or, come to think of it, your great-grandmother's house.

GUZINA OAXACA

Masaryk 513, Mexico City, **+52 55 5282 1820**
 www.guzinaoaxaca.com
CUISINE: Mexican
DRINKS: Full bar
SERVING: Breakfast, Lunch & Dinner
PRICE RANGE: $$
NEIGHBORHOOD: Polanco
Chef Alejandro Ruíz recently opened this location of
his acclaimed Oaxaca eatery serving contemporary
Mexican fare. Here you'll get delicious homemade
tortillas, tableside served Oaxacan salsa, and mole.
Great choice for breakfast. Make reservations for this
place.

LA BARRACA VALENCIANA

Centenario 91-C, Col. Del Carmen, Mexico City, +52
55 5658 1880

www.labarracavalenciana.com **WEBSITE DOWN AT PRESSTIME**
CUISINE: Spanish/Tapas/Small Plates
DRINKS: Beer & Wine Only
SERVING: Lunch & Dinner; closed Sun
PRICE RANGE: $$
NEIGHBORHOOD: Coyoacán
Small eatery (only 12 tables) serving a menu of tapas and small plates. Favorites include: Squid Roman, Grilled chicken breast and Chamorro veal. Specials change weekly.

LA CASA DE LAS SIRENAS
Calle Republica de Guatemala No. 32 Centro Histórico, Mexico City, +52 55 5704 3273
www.tortaslacastellana.com
CUISINE: Continental
DRINKS: Full Bar
SERVING: Breakfast, Lunch, Dinner
PRICE RANGE: $$$
NEIGHBORHOOD: Centro Histórico (Central Historic)
This charming restaurant overlooks the Cathedral of Mexico City and the National Palace. Menu favorites include: Roast chicken and Rib Eye. Delicious desserts. The restaurant features a tequila salon with dozens of agave spirits and a rooftop with tables that look into the cathedral's garden.

LA CASA DE TOÑO
Several Locations
Londres 144, + 52 55 5386 1125
https://m.lacasadetono.com.mx/

CUISINE: Mexican
DRINKS: Beer & Wine
SERVING: Open 24 hours (some vary)
PRICE RANGE: $
NEIGHBORHOOD: Juarez
Mexican diner open 24 hours. Very basic décor, nothing fancy. Large menu. Famous for its Pozole (which is a soup or stew with a base of hominy and mixed with meat (most often pork) and then finished off with seasonings and cabbage, lettuce, chili peppers, onion, garlic, radishes, avocado, or whatever they happen to decide that day. It's really flavorful. But the menu is quite vast—enchiladas, quesadillas, cochinita tacos, flan, rice pudding. Favorites: Pozole and Horchata. Mexican beers.

LA CASTELLANA

AV Revolucion 1309 esq Corregidora, Mexico City, +52 55 5593 5798
www.grupocastellano.com.mx
CUISINE: Mexican
DRINKS: Beer & Wine
SERVING: Lunch, Dinner
PRICE RANGE: $
Specializing in tortas, this is just one of five locations. The tortas are made with crisp-crusted and light bread, pickled jalapenos and a variety of fillings. And cheap, cheap, cheap.

LA DOCENA OYSTER BAR

Av. Álvaro Obregón 31, Mexico City, +52 55 5208 0833

www.ladocena.com.mx

CUISINE: Seafood

DRINKS: Full bar

SERVING: Lunch & Dinner

PRICE RANGE: $$$

NEIGHBORHOOD: Roma Norte

Seafood eatery specializing in oysters and barbecue. Favorite dish: Baby squid with garlic. Creative selection of desserts. Reservations recommended. English menu available.

LALO!

Calle Zacatecas 173, Mexico City, +52 55 5564 3388
www.eat-lalo.com
CUISINE: Breakfast/Pizza
DRINKS: Beer & Wine Only
SERVING: Breakfast, Lunch & Dinner; Lunch only
on Mon
PRICE RANGE: $$
NEIGHBORHOOD: Roma Norte
Chef Eduardo Garcia's casual eatery just across the
street from his more upscale eatery Maximo Bistrot.
Great choice for breakfast – have the French toast.
Amazing selection of pastries and house-made
yogurt. Dinner choices include dishes like freshly
made octopus with arugula.

LARDO

Agustín Melgar 6, Cuauhtemoc, Mexico City, +52 55 5211 7731

www.lardo.mx

CUISINE: French

DRINKS: Full bar

SERVING: Lunch & Dinner

PRICE RANGE: $$

NEIGHBORHOOD: Condesa

Hip eatery with a menu of Mexican and international cuisine. Great selection of seafood and seasonal dishes. They will even make dishes to order. Nice selection of wines.

LAS CAZUELAS DE LA ABUELA

Av San Jeronimo 630, Mexico City, +52 55 5683 8720

https://las-cazuelas-de-la-abuela.business.site

CUISINE: Mexican

DRINKS: Full Bar

SERVING: Dinner

PRICE RANGE: $

NEIGHBORHOOD: Pedregal

This family restaurant offers a menu of Mexican cuisine with Poblano overtones. The menu features 25 different stews and delicious peneques – a deep-fried quesadilla with green and red pumpkin-seed sauce.

LIMOSNEROS

Av. Ignacio Allende 3, Col. Centro Histórico, +52 55 5521 5576

http://limosneros.com.mx/

CUISINE: Mexican

DRINKS: Full Bar

SERVING: Lunch & Dinner

PRICE RANGE: $$$

NEIGHBORHOOD: Centro Norte

Upscale eatery offering Mexican cuisine with an international twist. The interior walls look like they were patched together using ancient stones. These walls are high and very dramatic. Interesting clear glass light fixtures dangle delicately from the high ceiling. Pots and vases on a shelf look like someone had a field day at a potter's shop. The lighting at night makes the place quite romantic. Bottles behind the bar are balanced (some of them precariously) on odd-shaped stone shelves. Has a menu including tacos, lamb, steak, Squid risotto and Crème Brule. My

favorites: the steak tacos. Nice wine list and tasty
cocktails.

LOS PANCHOS

Calle Tolstoi 9, Miguel Hidalgo, +52 55 5254 5430
www.lospanchos.mx
CUISINE: Mexican
DRINKS: Full bar
SERVING: Breakfast, Lunch & Dinner
PRICE RANGE: $$
NEIGHBORHOOD: Anzures
Great place for a family dinner.
Traditional Mexican eatery that's worth a try. Great
dishes and the steak here is exceptional (not your
typical American steak). Nice selection of desserts.

MAISON ARTEMISIA

Tonalá 23, Cuauhtémoc, Mexico City, +52 55 9036
3778
www.maisonartemisia.com
CUISINE: French
DRINKS: Full bar
SERVING: Lunch & Dinner; closed Sun
PRICE RANGE: $$$
NEIGHBORHOOD: Roma Norte
Upscale dining with an upstairs piano bar. Restaurant
offers a nice selection of seafood and beef. Favorites
include: Grilled octopus and Short-rib ravioli. This
place is famous for its imported absinthe and
absinthe-based cocktails.

MAXIMO BISTROT LOCAL

Tonalá 133, Mexico City, 52 55 5264 4291
www.maximobistrot.com.mx
CUISINE: Mexican, Italian, French
DRINKS: Wine
SERVING: Lunch, Dinner
PRICE RANGE: $$$$
NEIGHBORHOOD: Roma Norte
This rustic bistro, run by a young husband-and-wife team, offers a daily menu featuring ingredients found in the local markets. It has an open kitchen and has handwritten daily menus. Menu favorites include: Lamb loin and Tartar of Steelhead. Reservations required.

MERCADO ROMA COYOACAN

Miguel Angel Quevedo 353, Mexicto DF, 55 2155 9435
https://mrc.mercadoroma.com/
NEIGHBORHOOD: Coyoacán
Over 40 wildly diverse vendors occupy the 3 floors of this spectacular market, and a lot of them are eateries offering up authentic Mexican fare. While this is basically a collection of upscale food vendors that replicate the down-and-dirty street food you can find all over the city, in this place things are a little tidier, and the excitement stems from the fact that you can sample Mexican-fusion this or that, getting tastes from the far corners of this country. You can get tacos from 9 different regions of the country. But also elements of cuisine from around the world, all blended into Mexicsn cuisince. An Italian vendor serves tacos, but the taco is *piadina*, which is like a

tortilla, but comes from Italy. Hundreds of surprising
(and pleasing) combinations like this will enchant
you. If you're on a short visit, this place ought to be a
must, because you'll get to experience so much so
fast.

MERENDERO LAS LUPITAS

Plaza Santa Catarina 4, Col. Del Carmen, México,
D.F., +52 55 5554 3353
www.merenderolaslupitas.com.mx/
CUISINE: Mexican
DRINKS: No Booze
SERVING: Breakfast, Lunch; closed Mon & Tues
PRICE RANGE: $$
NEIGHBORHOOD: Coyoacán
Family-run eatery offering authentic Northern
Mexican fare. Try the atole (a corn based drink served

hot). Favorites: Chimichangas, egg & bean dishes and Flan.

MERO TORO

Calle Amsterdam 204, Mexico City, +52 55 5564 7799

www.merotoro.mx

CUISINE: Northern Mexican

DRINKS: Full Bar

SERVING: Dinner

PRICE RANGE: $$$

NEIGHBORHOOD: Condesa

Open since 2010, this eatery brings the surf-and-turf cuisine of Baja California to the Mexican highlands. Chef Jair Tellez created the expansive menu. Selections start with the small plate men featuring dishes like Ceviche ligero but don't forget the delicious main courses like Gently roasted grouper served on a bed of puréed cauliflower.

MOG

Frontera 168, Col. Roma, 52 55 5264 1629

CUISINE: Asian

DRINKS: Beer & Wine Only

SERVING: Lunch, Dinner

PRICE RANGE: $$

NEIGHBORHOOD: Roma Norte

This popular eatery offers a menu of sushi, Japanese style dishes and fusion. The bar serves a variety of Mexican and Japanese beers and sakes. Menu favorites include: Sushi rolls, Teriyaki Chicken and Yakimeshi. Desserts favorites include the green tea cake.

PASTELERÍA IDEAL
Several locations
16 de Septiembre No. 18, +52 55 5130 2970
Republic of Uruguay 74
Av. Hank González 773, Colonia Valle de Aragón
2nd. Sec.
https://www.pasteleriaideal.com.mx/
CUISINE: Bakery
DRINKS: No Booze
SERVING: 6:30 a.m. – 9:30 p.m.
PRICE RANGE: $
NEIGHBORHOOD: Centro Histórico de la Cdad.
Legendary bakery with endless aisles of breads,
cookies, croissants, cakes, and a variety of pastries
filled with ham & cheese, tuna, and other ingredients.
Worth a visit just to absorb the variety available. Plus,
it's a lot of fun to try pastry items you've never had
before. Eat in or take out. Cheap, too.

PASTELERIA LA GRAN VIA
Amsterdan 288-A, Mexico City, +52 55 5574 4008
www.pastelerialagranvia.com
CUISINE: Bakery/Specialty Grocery
NEIGHBORHOOD: Condesa
Popular bakery featuring a variety of breads, pastries, doughnuts, cakes and cookies. Great meringues and low-sugar options.

PUJOL
Tennyson 133, Mexico City, 52 55 5545 4111
www.pujol.com.mx
CUISINE: Mexican/Fusion
DRINKS: Full Bar
SERVING: Brunch, Lunch, Dinner
PRICE RANGE: $$$$
NEIGHBORHOOD: Polanco

With a reputation as one of the world's best restaurants (and hardest to get into with only a baker's dozen tables), this Mexican eatery mixes modern (mostly French-inspired) and ancient culinary techniques. Prix-fix menu. Menu favorites include: Fish ceviche taco and Fried pork belly. As an example of Chef Enrique Olvera's innovative culinary talents, I ordered tacos that had baby lamb, avocado-pera purée and the pungently aromatic herb, *hoja santa*. Delicious. This is why Olvera is Mexico's most famous chef.

QUINTONIL

Newton 55, Mexico City, +52 55 5280 2680
www.quintonil.com
CUISINE: Mexican
DRINKS: Full Bar
SERVING: Dinner
PRICE RANGE: $$$
NEIGHBORHOOD: Polanaco

This place takes traditional Mexican cuisine to the next level. Great margaritas and Mexican wines. Menu favorites include: Swiss chard tamale with raison puree; delicate slices of *chilacayote* squash and charred tortillas are topped with mole; *Huauzontle*, which is something similar to broccoli, is fried and served with salsa and cheese from Chiapas.

RESTAURANTE BAR CHON
Regina 160, 06090 México, D.F. +52 55 5542 0873
CUISINE: Mexican; Pre-Hispanic cuisine as well
DRINKS: Full bar
SERVING: Lunch & Dinner; closed Sunday
PRICE RANGE: $$$
NEIGHBORHOOD: Centro Sur
Traditional Mexican fare with most entrees based around the tortilla, rice and beans. This is one of the few places that also serves Pre-Hispanic food, so you can see what it was like to eat before Europeans arrived to muck it all up for the Indians. Unique offerings featuring insects, grasshoppers, worms, ant larvae and wild boar. Try the *pulque* ("blood of the gods"), a flavored beverage. A once-in-a-lifetime experience.

RESTAURANTE NICOS
Av. Cuitlahuac 3102, Mexico City, +52 55 5396 7090
www.nicosmexico.mx
CUISINE: Mexican
DRINKS: Full bar
SERVING: Breakfast, Lunch & Dinner; closed Sun
PRICE RANGE: $$$
NEIGHBORHOOD: Clavería

Not your typical Mexican eatery, great menu of "Nouvelle Mexican cuisine." Imaginative dishes and what many say is the "best" guacamole in the world. If you have a taste for sweets try the chocolate mousse cake. Menu in Spanish but the waiters do a good job of describing the dishes.
Good choice for breakfast.

ROKAI
Rio Ebro 87, Mexico City, +52 55 7826 1112
http://edokobayashi.com/index.php/rokai/
CUISINE: Japanese
DRINKS: Beer, Wine & Sake
SERVING: Lunch, Dinner; closed Sunday
PRICE RANGE: $
NEIGHBORHOOD: Cuauhtémoc
A favorite among locals and foodies, this small Japanese eatery serves up famous dishes like Rokai,

mussels sake, tuna, rib eye and duck, red snapper with
Himalayan salt and yuzu paste and Ensenada Octopus
sashimi. They also have a menu with nine or ten
courses –changing daily. They also have a real
standout menu item in their fried chicken. What
makes it different (and a delightful surprise for a
South Carolina boy like myself) is that it's marinated
in sake. The bar offers hot sake, green tea, Sapporo
beer and wine.

SUD777

Blvd. de la Luz 777, Col. Jardines del Pedregal,
México, D.F., +52 55 5568 4777
http://sud777.com.mx
CUISINE: Mexican
DRINKS: Full Bar
SERVING: Breakfast, Lunch, & Dinner
PRICE RANGE: $$$

NEIGHBORHOOD: Jardines del Pedregal
Great dining experience in a classic restaurant open since 2008 that offers cutting edge innovative cuisine while relying on traditional Mexican ingredients. Updated, modern, but still somehow traditional. The crisscrossing beams above give the place a modern look, as vines weave in and out of nooks and crannies. Light brown wooden tables mix with the blacks and grays to highlight the intimate décor. The chef swears he never uses any produce that's not Mexican. (I believe him.) There is a tasting menu, which I highly recommend. Be sure to get the wine pairing, because this place has one of the best selections of really local Mexican wines to be had in the city. Too many other upscale restaurants focus on foreign labels. Favorites: Tuna tostada with soy, Lechon pork, poblano chiles, Cotija cheese, a foie gras that's made locally and Crab ceviche. (There also a super good sushi bar, **Kokeshi**, tucked away inside this place.)

TABERNA DEL LEON

Altamirano 46, Col.Tizapán San Ángel, 01000
México, D.F., +52 55 5616 2110
www.tabernadelleon.rest
CUISINE: Mexican gourmet
DRINKS: Full bar
SERVING: Lunch & Dinner
PRICE RANGE: $$$$
NEIGHBORHOOD: San Angel
Beautiful upscale though casual eatery offering an exceptional dining experience. Favorites: Pork chop with Brussel sprouts and Foie gras; *robalo a los tres*

chiles (bass cooked with a three-pepper chili sauce). Excellent desserts like Chocolate cake served with raspberry ice cream.

TACOS DON JUAN
Atlixco 42, 06760 México, D.F., +52 55 5286 0816
No Website

CUISINE: Tacos
DRINKS: No Booze
SERVING: Lunch only
PRICE RANGE: $
NEIGHBORHOOD: La Condesa
Authentic hole-in-the-wall joint offering a rotating menu of fresh tacos. On Sunday, for instance, they'll serve tacos with *bistec con longaniza* (beef with sausage meat) topped off with a dollop of beans; on Friday or Saturday, you'll get *carnitas* (deep-fried pork). It doesn't matter what day you go, though, because every day the tacos are great, which accounts for the lines and why they've been here for so many years. Order at the counter – no inside seating, just outside.

TACOS EL HUEQUITO
Several Locations
Ayuntamiento 21, +52 55 5518 3313
Bolívar 58, Centro
Bajo Puente, Local 4 Esq. Juan Escutia, Col., Condesa
http://www.elhuequito.com.mx/
CUISINE: Mexican
DRINKS: No Booze
SERVING: Breakfast, Lunch, and Dinner
PRICE RANGE: $
NEIGHBORHOOD: Colonia Centro / Condesa
Taco stand located on a side street. Menu includes a variety of salsas and sauces for your tacos. But there's more to the menu—Gringas, Burritos, Nopalitos, Arabs, Aztec Soup, Corn Quesadillas (tasty). Food is served through a small window. Several locations

throughout the Central District, some with more generous seating available than the little hole in the wall I generally frequent.

TACOS MANOLO
Luz Saviñón 1305 (bet. Anaxágoras and Cauhtémoc), Mexico City, +52 55 7095 8071
No Website
CUISINE: Mexican
DRINKS:
SERVING: Lunch, Dinner
PRICE RANGE: $$
NEIGHBORHOOD: Colonia Del Valle
This busy stand is all about tacos. Try the classic Manolo, chopped bistec with onion and bacon.

TAQUERIA EL CALIFA
Altata 22, Mexico City, +52 55 5271 6285
www.elcalifa.com.mx

CUISINE: Mexican
DRINKS: Beer & Wine
SERVING: Dinner
PRICE RANGE: $$
NEIGHBORHOOD: Condesa
A popular taqueria with traditional favorites like the chicharon de queso and the Gaona conqueso.

TAQUERIA EL PROGRESO
Calle Maestro Antonio Caso 30, Col. Tabacalera, +52 55 5546 4700
https://taqueriaelprogreso.negocio.site/
WEBSITE DOWN AT PRESSTIME
CUISINE: Tacos
DRINKS: No Booze
SERVING: Breakfast, Lunch; closed Mon & Tues
PRICE RANGE: $
NEIGHBORHOOD: Tabacalera
Tacos at this great little sidewalk café are served with a variety of meats and lots of toppings including mashed potatoes, beans, cactus, manzanita peppers and onions. Cow head tacos served here (tacos de cabeza), as well as the excellent cow brain. (Check out the juice bar next door.)

TAQUERIA LOS COCUYOS

Calle Bolívar 56, Mexico City, 52 55 5518 4231
No Website
CUISINE: Tacos
DRINKS: Full Bar
SERVING: Lunch, Dinner
PRICE RANGE: $
NEIGHBORHOOD: Centro
This little taqueria offers up an interesting menu of tacos. Bright lights illuminate the different cuts of meat in a huge pan jammed with God knows what. You'd never stop at a place like this ordinarily. It's so small, so cramped, so scary looking. But it's the BEST. (The smell is so wonderful.) You tell them what you want and they cut the meat to order to make some of the best tacos you'll ever taste. And cheap, cheap, cheap. You eat standing in the street. Menu favorites include: Suadero (braised and seared beef) and Beef tongue taco.

TETETLAN

Av. de Las Fuentes 180, Col. Jardines del Pedregal, Ciudad de México, +52 55 5668 5335
https://tetetlan.com/restaurante/
CUISINE: Mexican
DRINKS: Full Bar
SERVING: Breakfast, Lunch, & Dinner

PRICE RANGE: $$
NEIGHBORHOOD: Pedregal
Located off the beaten path is this ultra-trendy eatery, that uses many different kinds of stone in its walls, rocks, bricks, poured concrete. Lots of weird angles, nooks and crannies. Completely charming. The name of this place actually means "place of many stones." You'll love it. They offer a menu of international and regional cuisine, boasting that over 90% of what they use comes from Mexico. Favorites: Roasted huitlacoche (this is a fungus that grows on corn), dried crickets with lemon and Tamales with hoja santa. Nice selection of tequilas.

TORTAS EL CAPRICHO
Augusto Rodin, 407, Mexico City, +52 55 3330 3935

CUISINE: Mexican
DRINKS: Beer & Wine
SERVING: Lunch, Dinner
PRICE RANGE: $
NEIGHBORHOOD: Colonia Mixoac
This eatery, very popular among the locals, specializes in tortas, large cake sandwiches, and offers nearly 50 varieties.

YUBAN

Colima 268, Mexico City, 52 55 6387 0358
www.yuban.mx
CUISINE: Mexican
DRINKS: Full Bar
SERVING: Lunch, Dinner
PRICE RANGE: $
NEIGHBORHOOD: Roma Norte
Chef Paloma Ortiz offers a menu featuring a variety of traditional recipes with a contemporary flair. There's a big emphasis on the *moles* from Oaxaca

Sierre Norte region. Menu favorites include: Smoky chichilo and the classic tlayuda. Desserts include a multi-dimensional multi-layer chocolate cake made with Oaxacan chocolate. At night the place becomes a hip hangout.

BALTRA
Iztaccíhuatl 36D, Cuauhtemoc, Mexico City, +52 55 5264 1279

www.baltra.bar

NEIGHBORHOOD: Condesa

Casual bar that offers a unique selection of cocktails – many created with tea leaves as one of the ingredients. Great selection of liquors.

Great comfortable bar with unique cocktails, knowledgeable bartenders and good design!

EL DEPÓSITO
Álvaro Obregón 21, Local 1, Mexico City, 52-55-5088-5552
www.eldeposito.com.mx
NEIGHBORHOOD: Condesa
This is part of a small chain of beer-bar-bottle shops that offer a wide selection of over 160 beers. Here you'll find a great selection of beer on tap, Mexican micros, European imports, German beers and a few Belgians. There's a terrace, TV, and free popcorn.

EL UNDER
Monterey 80, Col. Roma, 52 55 5511 5475
http://theunder.org/real/
NEIGHBORHOOD: Condesa
Another happening dance club.

FIFTY MILS
Paseo de la Reforma 500, Col. Juárez, México, D.F., +52 55 5230 1818
www.fiftymils.com
NEIGHBORHOOD: Juárez

Amazing quaint bar located in the **Four Seasons Hotel**. The Manhattan is their signature cocktail and it's top-notch. The bartenders are pros. But look closely at the "Creations" cocktail menu, which has cocktails unique to this wonderful lounge. Like Ant Man, which uses mescal, ants, egg whites, avocado, hoja santa bitters, soda water & lemongrass syrup. And that's just one cocktail! Plenty more to keep you busy. Hungry? Try the bar snacks like Grilled octopus with pineapple. Since you're here at the Four Seasons, try out the main restaurant, **IL BECCO**, featuring superior cuisine from the Piedmont region and a wondrous Italian wine list that will raise an eyebrow or two.

LA HERMOSA HORTENSIA
Callejón de la Amargura 4, Plaza Garibaldi 4, 52-55-5529-7828
No Website
NEIGHBORHOOD: Centro Norte

Located on the far corner of the Plaza Garibaldi, this pulquería is a must-stop for visitors. It's a 77-year old pulque bar that serves the lightly alcoholic Aztec drink, made from the maguey plant. The drink has the color of milk and comes in flavors like strawberry and coconut. This bar is included in the Museos Vivos project (which highlights "Living Museums"- every day venues that have cultural and historic significance).

LA NACIONAL
Orizaba 161, Mexico City, +52 55 5264 3106
No Website
NEIGHBORHOOD: Roma Norte
More of a bar than a restaurant with a very long list of Mexican microbrews. Great local hangout.

LICORERIA LIMANTOUR
Alvaro Obregon 106, Mexico City, +52 55 5264 4122
www.limantour.tv
NEIGHBORHOOD: Roma Norte
Popular bar that has been awarded the title as being "one of the best 50 bars in the world." Impressive cocktail list. Menu of bar snacks available – fries served with 4 different sauces.

M.N. ROY
Mérida 186, San Luis Potosi, 52 55 6681 0348
NEIGHBORHGOOD: Roma
www.mnroyclub.com
Emmanuel Picault opened this club and named it after the Indian revolutionary and founder of the Communist parties in both Mexico and India. It's super cool and gorgeously designed. Had throbbing house music late into the night. Dress to impress. It's a slick crowd here, even though the outside is designed to look like a simple ice cream parlor with a door the color of pink carnations.

PULQUERIA LOS INSURGENTES
Ave. de los Insurgentes Sur 226, Mexico City, +52 55 5207 0917
No Website

NEIGHBORHOOD: Roma Norte
Typical dive bar with loud music and sawdust on the floor. Multi-level bar including a dance floor. Menu of bar snacks. Live music and DJs on weekends. They serve flavored pulque -blended fresh juice mixed with tequila.

TÍO PEPE
Av Independencia 26, 01 55 5521 9136
https://cantina-el-tio-pepe.negocio.site/
PRICE RANGE: $$
NEIGHBORHOOD: Centro Poniente
Located in Chinatown area, this old cantina is a locals' favorite. How they can stand the harsh florescent lights pulsating a nasty white light right above their heads is beyond me. It would be a lot nicer if they'd turn off those damn lights, or put in something nicer with a dimmer switch. Maybe light a candle? I should stop bitching, because I somehow always end up here one way or another. A nice ornately carved back bar touting Hennessy Cognac

makes a stab providing some atmosphere. Simple menu of straight tequilas, brandies, rum and Cokes, and Fernets with soda. No food.

INDEX